THE CHOCOLATE THERAPIST™

Chocolate Remedies for a World of Ailments

Note for Librarians: a cataloguing record for this book that includes
Dewey Decimal Classification and US Library of Congress numbers
is available from the Library and Archives of Canada. The complete
cataloguing record can be obtained from their online database at:
www.collectionscanada.ca/amicus/index-e.html
ISBN 1-4120-4742-0
Printed in Victoria, BC, Canada

TRAFFORD

Offices in Canada, USA, Ireland, UK and Spain
This book was published on-demand in cooperation with Trafford
Publishing. On-demand publishing is a unique process and service of
making a book available for retail sale to the public taking advantage of
on-demand manufacturing and Internet marketing. On-demand publishing
includes promotions, retail sales, manufacturing, order fulfilment,
accounting and collecting royalties on behalf of the author.
Book sales for North America and international:
Trafford Publishing, 6E–2333 Government St.,
Victoria, BC v8t 4p4 CANADA
phone 250 383 6864 (toll-free 1 888 232 4444)
fax 250 383 6804; email to orders@trafford.com
Book sales in Europe:
Trafford Publishing (uk) Ltd., Enterprise House, Wistaston Road Business
Centre,
Wistaston Road, Crewe, Cheshire cw2 7rp UNITED KINGDOM
phone 01270 251 396 (local rate 0845 230 9601)
facsimile 01270 254 983; orders.uk@trafford.com

Order online at:
www.trafford.com/robots/04-2550.html

10 9 8

www.thechocolatetherapist.com

There are two types of people in the world—
those who love chocolate and those who
will soon. Perhaps this is why philosophers
originally coined the phrase "we are all one."
Once you understand the concept, life
becomes considerably easier.

I dedicate this book to you:
The chocolate lovers
of the world.

DISCLAIMER

The author releases all responsibility to those choosing to self-medicate with chocolate. Although the research is factual, the book is not intended to be used in place of a physician's prescriptions or recommendations. However, if you've come to positive conclusions while testing your tolerance for chocolate under controlled (and even uncontrolled) circumstances, please share your discoveries with the author. Your research may contribute to a future remedy for devoted chocolate souls everywhere.

e-mail address: docchoc@thechocolatetherapist.com

CONTENTS

INTRODUCTION

A few short decades ago smoking was harmless and cool, drinking a glass of red wine a day was the sign of a problem drinker and eating carbohydrates was the best way to lose weight. Even chocolate was considered bad for you. Fortunately those days are behind us. We now know that smoking causes cancer, a daily glass of red wine can prolong your life and the best way to lose weight is by following a low-carb diet. But the most exciting news is that "chocolate" and "healthy" can finally be used in the same sentence. The Age of Chocolate has arrived!

With research results still coming in, many people are wondering how chocolate, a food on the "diet-don't" list for years, can be healthy. Yet surprisingly chocolate contains a wide variety of benefits for the body including endorphins, mood-lifting neurotransmitters and a delightful collection of flavor compounds. It also contains a healthy supply of vitamins and minerals. You can even eat chocolate daily without gaining weight!

Perhaps all this seems too good to be true. I doubted it myself until a simple event triggered a full scale investigation. While I was deleting a collection of "highly important" e-mail ads for Viagra, weight-loss pills and guaranteed depression cures, I came across a single enticing message entitled "Why Chocolate is Good for You." When I opened it I discovered the following interesting facts: 1) Chocolate has more antioxidants by weight than red wine. 2) Chocolate releases endorphins into the brain that have been proven to uplift moods and reduce the sensation of pain. 3) Chocolate contains over 400 flavor compounds and chemicals that all benefit the body in some way. The list went on and the news got better with every sentence. As I surveyed the layout of information on my computer screen more closely, I realized that the e-mail for chocolate had arrived directly between the advertisements of our most pressing health issues. Having reviewed the informative essentials, I began to theorize: Wouldn't it be convenient if chocolate could solve our health problems? Being a devout chocolate connoisseur, I set out to justify my passion. The investigation began immediately.

The internet, libraries, newspapers and trade journals all heralded praises for chocolate. At parties, the mere mention of the word "chocolate" started a swirl of highly intriguing conversations. At the check-out stand, curious strangers in line poured forth elixir-like tales of chocolate while I purchased stacks of bars for additional research. Numerous friends leaped in with personal stories about how they used chocolate to self medicate. A pharmacist friend even declared that if the highly complex cocoa bean were discovered today, it would probably be regulated by the Food and Drug Administration. It seemed that more information on the abundant health benefits of chocolate unveiled before me every day. And of course everyone I talked to wanted to see the facts so they could justify their indulgences.

The investigation expanded to other foods commonly added to chocolate bars such as nuts, dried fruits and berries, cinnamon, vanilla, ginger, cranberries, spices and even espresso. This new information revealed additional encouraging facts about food and health. The growing inventory of positive research pointed to the obvious fact that exercising the choice to eat real foods (rather than processed) guarantees significant health benefits.

Of course, some people may not define the chocolate bar as a non-processed food. But once I'd considered the research, I determined that it's possible to eat chocolate in a form that's quite close to the original cocoa bean. And it's actually a fruit, so eating chocolate provides many of the same benefits as eating fruit. The key then is to eat the "right" kind of chocolate~but what exactly does that mean?

It turns out that the "right" kind of chocolate contains at least 50% cocoa solids or more. Cocoa solids are cocoa beans reduced down to their purest form. The process requires roasting the beans to release the shells, grinding them into a cocoa liquor, heating and pressing the liquor to remove most of the cocoa butter, and finally grinding the cooled solids into powder. Because it's so bitter, the powder is used as an ingredient in foods and not eaten alone. A high quality bar includes at least half of its ingredients from cocoa solids. Good tasting chocolate might contain less, but ideally it should be at least 50% cocoa to get the most health value.

Since the beneficial elements of chocolate are within the bean, it makes sense that the higher the cocoa content, the greater the nutrient value. High quality chocolate bars should contain no less than 50% cocoa, but unfortunately these bars aren't just lying around at the average check out stand. You have to seek them out.

One of the first (and worst) places we all look is the candy aisle of the average grocery store, home to a selection so vast it could take hours to make a decision. Chocolate containing the highest levels of fat and sugar crowd the candy shelves throughout the United States. But fortunately this picture is beginning to change. Increased awareness of chocolate's health benefits and a growing demand for high quality chocolate has brought many excellent brands into the market just within the last ten years. Some of the best places to find the quality bars are natural food stores and the internet (see Appendix B). An internet search for "high quality dark chocolate" yields over 700,000 websites devoted to chocolate. With these kinds of choices at your fingertips there's no excuse for not finding the perfect quality chocolate to suit your every whimsical mood.

Always keep in mind that the darker the chocolate, the higher the health benefits. Milk chocolate lovers are advised to add a bit of dark chocolate into their diets with the goal of developing a taste for this hearty and healthy confection. To help your palate make the conversion from milk to dark chocolate as simple and painless as possible, refer to the section in the book called "Going to the Dark Side."

The Chocolate Therapist is divided into easy-to-follow sections so you can get the facts quickly and move directly to the chocolate remedies.

•A **Brief History:** Unique and entertaining facts that can be used at any social gathering.

•**Healthy Investigation:** An overview of the extraordinary health benefits of chocolate.

•**Selecting the Proper Chocolate:** Learn how to choose the best chocolate for optimal health and become an expert in your field.

•**Proper Chocolate Consumption:** Quickly acquire the tasting skills of a distinguished chocolate connoisseur.

•**Self Diagnose, Self Medicate:** Learn how to use chocolate to help alleviate an assortment of health issues.

More studies are currently being conducted than ever before devoted to discovering chocolate's many hidden values. I'm even conducting a rather promising investigation of my own. I've started recommending to my children that they eat dark chocolate instead of other snacks. The results so far? As predicted~they're taking to the idea rather well.

For myself, whenever I give in to the dessert tray I now opt for a chocolate selection. In the past I mulled over every possible dessert. Now I simply decide which chocolate delicacy to enjoy. In the event that there are more than one, it's easy to convince someone else at the table to order one while I select the other. Between the two

of us, we enjoy the broadest range of "health benefits."
Now please take a moment to learn the basics, then off
to chocolate therapy you go!

A BRIEF HISTORY

In the late 1400's, Columbus brought the cocoa bean back to Spain from his travels. However, the tiny bean was overshadowed by the vast collection of larger treasures he arrived with at the same time. Nothing became of it until Cortez reintroduced it nearly three decades later on returning to Spain from South America.

In 1516, the Aztecs introduced Cortez to cocoa. The "xocolatl" (as it was termed at the time) was consumed primarily as a drink without sugar and it was quite bitter. The Aztecs honored chocolate as a "food of the Gods" and it was highly esteemed within their society. They revered the drink to such an extent that often the solid gold goblets used to drink the cocoa at festivals were thrown away after just one use. Montezuma reportedly took goblets of the drink before attending to his harem, giving cocoa its much touted reputation as an aphrodisiac. The cocoa bean itself was used as money and it was quite worthy~just four little beans could purchase a tur-key.

Cocoa was clearly as valuable as it was diverse, and Cortez was intrigued by its economic potential. So when he returned to Spain in 1528, he re-introduced chocolate to the royal court of King Charles. Initially the Spaniards didn't like its bitterness. Yet with his first hand under-standing of cocoa's value and magical allure, Cortez was determined to convince the court of its significance. He and his men tried adding sugar, vanilla and various spic-es to the drink. After experimenting with a few different combinations, they finally came up with a product that everyone seemed to enjoy. When someone realized a short time later that the drink tasted much better served hot, chocolate's popularity caught on very quickly.

But rather than share their new secret with the world, the Spanish court decided to keep it for their private use. Cocoa rapidly became the preferred beverage of Spanish aristocracy. Remarkably, the Spaniards kept the knowledge of the chocolate industry from the rest of the continent for nearly a century. Finally in 1606, Ital-ian explorer Antonio Carletto "rediscovered" chocolate once again and introduced it to other parts of Europe. At the same time, Spain's power was in decline and the secret of chocolate began to leak out. The chocolate revolution had begun.

Chocolate was first introduced in the United States in 1765 when cocoa beans were brought from the West Indies to Dorchester, Massachusetts. The John Harmon Company is credited with producing the first chocolate in the US, primarily marketed for its medicinal values. But chocolate's notable presence was established well over a century later. In 1894, a young man by the name of Milton Hershey founded the first chocolate factory in the United States, the Hershey Chocolate Company.

Mr. Hershey got his start using chocolate to coat the caramels he was already manufacturing. Realizing that a sweeter type of chocolate would be a better compliment to his caramels, he experimented with milk chocolate. This new, lighter version of the original treat turned out to be immensely popular with consumers because of its mild and creamy taste. Within a relatively short period of time, Hershey had revolutionized the future of chocolate. Not only had he created a chocolate that appealed to nearly everyone's taste, but he'd figured out a way to mass produce it in a variety of products such as bars and wafers. In doing this, he effectively lowered the price and made it available to people of all income levels. Chocolate was well on its way to becoming one of the country's most popular snacks.

Today, the average American consumes just over 12 pounds of chocolate per year. Although that may sound like a mountain of chocolate, it averages out to one pound of chocolate per month, or one candy bar every three days. After some careful calculating, it may have occurred to you that you've been consuming more than your fair share of the quota. If so, you could be drawing from your international heritage. The list below shows a few of the world's more committed chocolate consuming countries.

Switzerland	23 lbs/yr per person
Ireland	20 lbs/yr
Norway	18 lbs/yr
United Kingdom	18 lbs/yr
Australia	13 lbs/yr

Although a few questionable articles may have been written about chocolate over the years, they don't appear to have kept people from eating it! And as recent articles pop up with titles like "Chocolate: The New Health Food," there's never been a better time to restock the cupboards with chocolate. I propose that at some point chocolate should be added to the new food pyramid, right next to its culinary cousins, the fruits. After all, it's good for you. Keep following along to find how just how good it is....

HEALTHY INVESTIGATION

Chocolate is blessed with large quantities of antioxidants, also called flavinoids, catechins and polyphenols. Antioxidants are media darlings because of their extraordinary health-enhancing properties. Their most significant benefit is their ability to block the formation of free radicals~destructive chains of incomplete molecules that damage the body and cause a variety of illnesses, including heart disease and cancer. Eating foods that are high in antioxidants helps the body fight free radicals and also assists the entire immune system in combating many illnesses.

Antioxidants come in a variety of forms. The most popular and easy to consume are vitamins such as A, C, E, CoQ10, alpha lipoic acid and selenium. You can also get considerable antioxidants from drinking green tea or red wine, and eating fruits and vegetables. Where does chocolate fit in? Of all food choices, chocolate has one of the highest levels of antioxidants per gram. Studies have shown that one dark chocolate bar provides twice the antioxidant benefit as drinking a glass of red wine.

If you really want to get serious about increasing antioxidants, add unsweetened cocoa powder to your diet. It contains two times the level of antioxidants as standard dark chocolate. While I wouldn't suggest adding cocoa powder to your morning coffee, take a look at the information in Appendix C. It contains a short collection of excellent recipes using plenty of free radical-fighting dark chocolate. You might also want to investigate Starbuck's delightful new Chantico,™ a special drinking chocolate made from cocoa powder, cocoa butter and steamed milk. You can throw in a little extra cocoa powder for maximum nutritional value.

What about the fat in chocolate? Fortunately it's not nearly as detrimental as once suspected. Peter Laret, author of *Three Cheers for Chocolate*, reports that much of the fat in chocolate is actually cholesterol-friendly fat. Approximately one-third of it is stearic acid and another third is oleic acid, both considered "good fats" because they don't raise cholesterol levels. To maximize "good fat" intake, consume brands with a high percentage of cocoa solids~50% or more. Many of the preferred chocolate manufacturers (see Appendices A & B) include this information on the label. But if you're in doubt, visit the manufacturer's website usually listed on the wrapper (see Appendix A for a list of recommended websites).

What we've intuitively known for centuries is finally becoming scientific fact, and it appears that the good news is just starting. After reading through the research you'll conclude for yourself just what you've always hoped to be true—chocolate is truly good for you.

SELECTING THE PROPER CHOCOLATE

While it's true that eating chocolate offers many health benefits, it's also true that one can enjoy too much of a good thing. The majority of chocolate consumed by Americans is loaded with a huge percentage of sugar and fat. Rather than grabbing the quickest bar in sight, follow these simple guidelines to assure the most nutritional value from your chocolate selection.

Dark chocolate is better for you than milk chocolate and milk chocolate is far superior to white chocolate. So it's healthiest to make your chocolate choice as dark as tolerable. Fortunately it's not as difficult as it once was to find the type of chocolate that offers the maximum nutritional benefits. Cocoa-loving baby boomers have increased the demand for quality chocolate, and this drive is creating a larger variety of "healthy" chocolate on the market than ever before. The chocolates containing the highest level of cocoa are the healthiest. Once again, those with 50% or more cocoa solids are considered quality chocolates. Most dark quality chocolate bars contain 55-73% cocoa solids, easily meeting the standards for healthy chocolate. They offer an abundance of nutrients per gram and far less sugar and fat than lower quality bars. If you're skeptical, just compare a list of the nutrients in 100g of dark chocolate with the side of your vitamin bottle (see Vitamin Deficiency in the "Prescriptions" section for a complete chart of the nutrients in dark chocolate). You may be surprised to see how many vitamins and minerals are contained in just one bar.

Obviously it's best to avoid chocolates with minimal cocoa content. Many of the mainstream brands contain less than 20% cocoa and some even get down to as low as 7% cocoa. When a chocolate bar contains only 7% cocoa, the remaining 93% of the bar is primarily sugar and fat~the nemesis of the true chocolate connoisseur. Undoubtedly, this is why chocolate picked up its unfavorable reputation. But by selecting brands with the highest percentage of cocoa, you keep sugar and fat intake to a reasonable minimum.

It's also a good idea to avoid consuming chocolates with gooey, enticing centers. Most filled chocolates are very high in sugar. Eating all that sugar definitely outweighs the benefits of the surrounding chocolate. An excellent example is the popular cream-filled chocolate which contains almost 100% sugar.

The boxed chocolate enthusiast should consider acquiring a taste for healthier chocolate. It may require a carefully monitored program, but just keep your health in mind as you make the move and take it one day at a time. However, if you know you absolutely can't exist without filled chocolates, try this website: www.aphrodite-chocolates.co.uk. This company offers a variety of "healthier" filled chocolates so you can indulge and still obtain a few benefits.

While going dark is the first component of proper chocolate selection, choosing "organic" is also important. The first reason is obvious: When cocoa beans are grown free from chemicals and pesticides, these harmful additives won't be passed on to your body. But there's another reason to consider as well.

The demand for higher quality chocolate has recently increased substantially. Unfortunately this trend has caused cocoa growers (particularly on the Ivory Coast in Africa) to pay their workers wages far below poverty levels. Some of these growers also use very young children as field laborers.

Organic chocolate, on the other hand, is typically not manufactured by companies where these appalling labor situations exist. Since organic growers are able to charge more for their cocoa, they generally pay their workers higher wages and also refrain from using children as laborers. (For complete information on this topic, please refer to *Chocolate Unwrapped* by Rowan Jacobson.)

Once you weigh the pros and cons, there's hardly a reason not to buy organic. You'll get superior quality chocolate, more antioxidants, no pesticides, and you'll support those who labor to bring you the delights you love. When you consider the cost of a double latte devoid of nutritional value, the cost of a vitamin-packed organic chocolate bar suddenly becomes a bit more reasonable. So for the sake of your health as well as supporting a politically correct chocolate industry, why not spend a little more for top quality chocolate?

PROPER CHOCOLATE CONSUMPTION

Have you ever considered whether you eat chocolate properly? I'd been a devout consumer for decades and the thought had never entered my mind. Well you'll be relieved to learn that there are published guidelines to assist with just such a task. Once I'd read them I realized I'd been doing it wrong all along! Fortunately it was evident that having an imperfect technique didn't appear to affect either my love for chocolate or how much I enjoyed every indulgence. Yet once I started using the correct procedure, it made all the difference. Even if you have your own technique perfected, take a moment to evaluate this quick review to make sure you aren't missing anything critical.

According to the American Dietetic Association (ADA), a person should observe the following guidelines when eating chocolate to insure the maximum pleasurable benefits:

First of all, chocolate tastes best when eaten on an empty stomach. In the event that you ever find you have an empty stomach, this could be the perfect time to enjoy a little indulgence. I noticed the guidelines failed to mention what would happen if you didn't have an empty stomach. Conveniently, through personal research I concluded that regardless of the condition of your stomach, chocolate can be eaten without any negative side effects. (However, if you have ulcers, do not eat chocolate on an empty stomach as it's been reported to occasionally aggravate this condition.)

Next, chocolate should be eaten in order of the amount of cocoa it contains. It's best to start with the confections containing the least amount of cocoa. The cocoa taste is quite concentrated, so starting with dark chocolate can overpower your taste buds. Always enjoy your white chocolate first (which has no cocoa in it at all), followed by milk chocolate and finally dark chocolate.

Perhaps you're planning to attend a chocolate tasting festival. (You may even want to concoct a 10 course sampling in the privacy of your own home.) It could be disastrous to eat the chocolate out of order~you might not fully benefit from the many varied flavors of the feast. So remember: white chocolate, then milk chocolate, and finally dark chocolate.

Now you're ready to begin the actual tasting. Pick up the chocolate and observe it as you would a work of fine art, taking time to examine its beauty and perfection. This step should last anywhere from 10 to 30 seconds. The anticipation of your encounter will increase the overall sensation. (If you're eating a chocolate bar, break off an individual bite size piece.) Gently wave the chocolate before your nose, inhaling the tantalizing aroma while appreciating the many flavor compounds you're about to experience.

Slowly slide the chocolate into your mouth, allowing your lips to sense the gentle softness of the chocolate's texture. Let it sit in your mouth for a few seconds and begin to melt. Conveniently, chocolate melts just below body temperature, so this phase begins immediately. As you start chewing, swirl the chocolate around with your tongue to all four of its taste zones—front, back, and side to side. The tongue's four zones differentiate an array of tastes~salt, sour, bitter and sweet~so the chocolate will stimulate unique flavor sensations in each zone.

You may continue chewing as you swirl, but don't swallow just yet. Take a moment to press the chocolate onto the roof of your mouth, savoring one last moment of melting and flavored euphoria. Relax, breathe deep and take in the lingering cacophony of sensations. Once you've completed this final step of delicious enjoyment, swallow at last.

Before indulging in your next delicacy, rinse your palate thoroughly with water, coffee or wine to prepare it for the ensuing unique experience. When ready, move to the next confection for another go around, repeating the process exactly as previously defined. You may stop when you've reached the necessary level of satiation or all of the chocolate is gone, whichever comes first.

Keep in mind that even if you've been eating chocolate incorrectly for years no harm will come of it. My own technique involved moving directly from sliding the chocolate into my mouth (although not slowly, as advised) to cleansing my palate in preparation for the next confection. The idea that there could be 15 missing steps was completely foreign. Of course it's never too late to change. Once you've started making step-by-step adjustments you may realize that some of those steps are rather valuable. Pass the wine, please.

SELF-DIAGNOSE, SELF-MEDICATE

For years I attempted to contain my chocolate habit through abstinence, an effort that proved to be extremely agonizing at times. So imagine my delight when I first realized that chocolate has the power to heal. It didn't take long to make sure every conceivable problem was addressed properly!

The premise is very simple—find your ailment and follow the recommended chocolate prescription. It's best to use a little common sense while self-medicating. If you suffer from a host of problems, it won't do much good to try and resolve everything at once. Although having a little chocolate is healthy, eating 10 of the recommended bars in a single day is likely to induce an entire new set of disorders you may not be prepared to address. Choose the most pressing issue and work from there.

The ailments are alphabetized, then divided into three parts: "Prescriptions," "Recommended Bars" and "Supporting Evidence." The "Prescriptions" consist of chocolate bars with an assortment of different ingredients, all carefully considered to help alleviate your ailment. The "Recommended Bars" are a collection of quality chocolate options that support the prescription and also contain superior nutrients. The "Supporting Evidence" section presents scientific facts gathered from current research supporting how chocolate can assist with the ailment at hand. Most of the prescriptions call for dark chocolate, but I've recommended a few milk chocolate selections for the sake of variety. But always remember that darker chocolate offers more nutritional benefits.

You may become completely healthy and have no further need to consult the book. If so, consider following a preventative program of eating a small collection of healthy chocolates every day. (Unfortunately insurance companies are not covering this new pre-emptive health care plan at this time.) And don't just let your inquiry stop with this book. Keep up with the experts who are continually researching the many benefits of chocolate. It's quite possible that the best is yet to come.

It's likely that your extraordinary new outlook on chocolate will prove monumentally beneficial. People will wonder why you're looking so radiant and demand to know what you're doing. You may even become the life of the party. And with your new and astonishing knowledge surrounding the benefits of one of the world's most loved foods, you'll save countless others from a lifetime of deprivation that could very well take a year off their life (see "Life Expectancy"). So here's to your health!

PRESCRIPTIONS

It's finally time to apply all of this information to your health. Each prescription includes a chocolate bar, often with added ingredients or additional steps to help speed your revival. The recommended chocolate bars noted after each of the prescriptions are suggestions and not requirements. Feel free to replace your favorite bar wherever it's appropriate. Now let's eat chocolate!

ALLERGIES

Prescription: Take 2 squares dark or milk organic chocolate, every 6 hours as needed while drinking Yogi® Ginger Tea. Do not exceed 12 squares in any 24 hour period. Children under 12 should take half the dose.

Recommended bar: Dagoba® milk chocolate with ginger and chai or Dagoba® dark chocolate with lavender and blueberry.

SUPPORTING EVIDENCE

Chocolate contains theobromine which has recently been shown to offer the same cough suppressing advantages as codeine (see prescription for "cough"). The ginger in both the tea and the recommended bar will offer significant relief as well. Ginger contains anti-inflammatory properties and has long been used by traditional healers to help control a variety of health problems including allergies and other respiratory conditions. It's a natural antihistamine as well as a decongestant, and it dilates constricted bronchial tubes offering relief to the sufferer.

Allergic to chocolate? In a study of 81 people who believed they were allergic to chocolate, researchers found only one person with an actual chocolate allergy. According to a prominent allergist at the National Jewish Medical Research Center in Denver, in thirty years of allergy testing for chocolate they found less than thirty-five cases of actual chocolate allergies. It's quite possible that people try to convince themselves that they're allergic to chocolate merely as an excuse to stay away from it~certainly a self-torture we should avoid at every expense. Of course if you're positively allergic to chocolate, you may want to pass this book on to a friend.

ANEMIA

Prescription: 4 squares dark chocolate with almonds taken on an empty stomach, or any other time you feel like taking it, up to a maximum of 16 squares in a given day. Optional: 10 additional almonds (without chocolate) taken at any time.

Recommended bar: Tropical Source® toasted almond dark chocolate bar

SUPPORTING EVIDENCE

Anemia is a condition in which the level of red blood cells in the bloodstream falls to a very low level. Without enough red cells, the body is unable to carry the oxygen needed to maintain healthy tissues and organs. Iron helps build red blood cells, and a deficiency in this mineral can lead to anemia. Eating foods rich in iron can help reduce the possibility of becoming anemic.

A quality bar of dark chocolate provides approximately 7.5% of your daily iron requirement. Adding 3.5 oz of almonds to the mix brings the total up to 29%, and almonds perform double duty. Not only do they boost the daily iron percentage but they also contain copper (approximately 1.15mg per 100g), which, when combined with the vitamins and iron in chocolate, acts as a catalyst for the formation of new blood cells. If you're really feeling industrious, melt the chocolate and almonds together (on very low heat) in an iron pot. Research has shown that cooking in iron pots raises the iron content of the food.

ANTi-WRiNKLE ASSiSTANCE

Prescription: 6 squares dark organic chocolate taken one at a time with a glass of red wine. Enjoy at home with an invitation-only spa party with the girls, guys or both. Apply organic dark chocolate mask, as instructed on the box. Entertaining movie optional. Repeat monthly.

Recommendations: Godiva® sugar free dark chocolate bar; Ecco Bella™ organic dark chocolate mask

SUPPORTING EVIDENCE

The recent explosion of chocolate-based skincare products confirms that chocolate's use is no longer limited to the stomach. It's now acceptable for the face and body as well.

Perhaps you're questioning the logic behind applying chocolate to the face as it's rumored to cause acne. But just like everything else in life, correct application is the key. Here are just a few of the facts, quoted directly from the recommended Ecco Bella™ mask box: "....this chocolate mask treatment is naturally pure and rich in iron, magnesium, vitamins and antioxidants.....these nutrients nourish and cleanse your skin while leaving it softer and smoother than ever." When you participate with a group of friends, you'll get the fabulous benefit of laughing hysterically when you see how lovely everyone looks in their fresh and skin-friendly dark chocolate mask.

After the cleansing mask, you might want to apply Origins new cocoa therapy™ Deeply nourishing body butter. Just like the mask, this product is loaded with vitamins, minerals and more wrinkle-fighting antioxidants. After testing their product on 53 volunteers, Origins reported that 74% of the participants said they actually felt happier after experiencing it for just 10 minutes. It appears that some of chocolate's benefits can be enjoyed without so much as single calorie gain! The product also contains the aromatic and enchanting scents of vanilla, ginger and orange, all specifically added to ensure your state of relaxed euphoria.

When you choose the recommended bar, you'll enjoy Godiva's® wonderful sugar-free dark chocolate. It's certainly acceptable to choose regular Godiva® chocolate as well. Just keep in mind that the darker your selection, the more health benefits you'll receive. Either way, you'll be getting a delicious dose of wrinkle-fighting antioxidants. Now off you go to the spa.

ANTIOXIDANT ASSISTANCE

Prescription: 8 squares dark organic chocolate taken throughout the day; repeat daily as you wish, up to a maximum of 2.5 oz of chocolate in a 24 hour period.

Recommended bar: Terra Nostra™ organic intense dark chocolate: 73% cocoa

SUPPORTING EVIDENCE

Antioxidants, polyphenols and catechins: All powerful aides to the body and all abundantly available in dark chocolate. Antioxidants assist the body by working against oxidation (the breakdown of tissues). Polyphenols are naturally occurring chemicals heavily present in green tea and are considered to be very powerful antioxidants. They've been touted for their aide in preventing heart disease and cancer. Catechins, a class of polyphenols, also have very potent antioxidant capabilities. Like polyphenols, catechins are generally found in green tea, but chocolate lovers will rejoice in the fact that a bar of dark chocolate contains twice as many catechins as a cup of green tea.

Eating a high content dark chocolate bar is like swallowing a snack stuffed with these powerful antioxidants. Whether you're counting flavonoids, catechins or polyphenols, gram for gram dark chocolate comes out above or near the top every time.

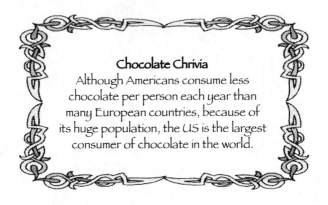

Chocolate Chrivia
Although Americans consume less chocolate per person each year than many European countries, because of its huge population, the US is the largest consumer of chocolate in the world.

ARTHRITIS

Prescription: 4 squares dark organic chocolate with or without hazelnuts every 4 hours, as needed to reduce pain and increase chocolate euphoria. Take with or without meals. Maximum intake of 12 squares in any 24 hour period.

Recommended bar: Rapunzel's semisweet bar with hazelnuts

SUPPORTING EVIDENCE

Scientists have recently discovered that polyphenols, heavily present in chocolate, significantly reduce the possibility of getting some forms of arthritis. Polyphenols contain anti-inflammatory properties and that could help explain the connection between chocolate consumption and reduced arthritic inflammation. A bar with nuts is recommended because nuts assist with calcium absorption and prevent the body from becoming calcium deficient. Studies have shown that arthritic conditions worsen where calcium deficiencies are present.

ASTHMA

Prescription: Take one half of a dark organic chocolate bar with one cup of peppermint tea. Read a good book, repeat as necessary until you feel better. Maximum one bar per day.

Recommended Bar: Organic Swiss dark chocolate bar.

SUPPORTING EVIDENCE

Asthma is a respiratory disorder generally thought to be caused by an allergic reaction involving immune system dysfunction. When under attack, the body releases histamines to combat foreign substances like dust, pollen and some types of food. In an over-responsive body, histamines cause an excessive rush of blood and lymph fluid to the affected area, causing an inflammation of the lungs and impeding breathing.

Chocolate contains a chemical called proanthocyanidin which is an anti-inflammatory. Proanthocyanidin is used in vitamins and medicines that are specially formulated for assisting in arthritis, another inflammatory disease. The proanthocyanidin in chocolate actually helps block the body's release of histamines which can help reduce the side effects of an asthmatic allergic reaction. The small amount of caffeine in chocolate may be beneficial as well. Caffeinated foods and beverages can help dilate bronchial tubes and make breathing easier.

Peppermint tea helps clear breathing passages as well. Peppermint oil has been used for centuries as a decongestant because it relaxes nasal passages and even reduces pain. It's regularly found in cough syrups, ointments, nasal decongestants and inhalants. But why go to all that medicinal trouble? You can enjoy many of the same benefits by simply eating a mint chocolate bar and drinking a cup of mint tea.

BLOOD SUGAR CONTROL

Prescription: 4 squares dark organic chocolate with or without almonds, hazelnuts, or pecans, taken with 8 oz. water or skim milk. Take after the lunch and dinner meals.

Recommended bar: Dagoba® organic milk chocolate with espresso and cinnamon, or Chocolove® dark chocolate w/almonds and cherries.

SUPPORTING EVIDENCE

There's certainly no way to advocate the use of chocolate to control blood sugar. However, there's an appropriate time to eat chocolate that won't do much to affect your triglycerides, or blood sugar levels. While it's true that chocolate supposedly tastes better on an empty stomach (see Proper Chocolate Consumption), it's not the ideal way to eat chocolate when attempting to keep blood sugar stabilized. The key is to eat it after a meal, preferably where you've eaten a healthy portion of protein (20 grams or more). Protein acts as a stabilizer for blood sugar because it's absorbed into the bloodstream very slowly. It balances foods that cause blood sugar to rise such as sugars and processed carbohydrates. And although a 100g chocolate bar contains four grams of protein, you're still better off eating chocolate after a protein-rich meal.

Chocolate also contains chromium which is a mineral associated with controlling blood sugar. Adding chromium to the daily diet has proven to increase glucose metabolism in as little as 4-6 weeks. It may even assist with increasing your ability to properly metabolize cholesterol.

Nuts also help keep blood sugar levels low. Nuts contain fat, and like protein, fat helps reduce the rate at which sugar is absorbed into the bloodstream. If you had a choice between eating a bowl of processed cereal (any brand) or an organic dark chocolate bar, the chocolate bar would be a much healthier option when considering blood sugar control. Nearly every processed cereal raises blood sugar substantially, while a chocolate bar with nuts comes in quite low at 34 on the glycemic index scale. (See appendix D for a brief description of the glycemic index and how it works.)

Although the recommended Dagoba® bar doesn't contain nuts, it would be a good idea to consume a handful of almonds or some other type of nuts along with the bar for the benefits listed above. I recommend this Dagoba® bar because it contains cinnamon. Recent research on cinnamon indicates that it helps lower blood sugar. The study, performed on 60 individuals with type 2 diabetes, confirmed that 1/4 tsp of cinnamon given twice daily reduced both blood sugar levels and bad cholesterols.

Finally, both chocolate and cinnamon contain proan-thocyanidin, the ingredient that appears to activate the insulin receptor in cells. More than one study has confirmed that cinnamon enhances insulin action and may be beneficial in controlling blood glucose levels and diabetes.

CAFFEINE WITHDRAWAL

Prescription: 1.2 oz bar dark organic chocolate any time of day with a cup of coffee or caffeinated beverage of your choice. Limit one chocolate bar per day.

Recommended bar: Newman's Own® organic sweet dark chocolate with espresso—available in both 1.2 oz and 2.8 oz sizes

SUPPORTING EVIDENCE

Chocolate has long been credited as a pick-me-up food because it contains caffeine. But it's most likely the sugar, endorphins, vitamins and minerals in chocolate that do the picking up and not the caffeine. The amount of caffeine in chocolate is insignificant. Unless you're eating plenty of high quality unsweetened baking chocolate, you won't really be able to use chocolate to help stay awake. For that quick pick-me-up, it's better to include a caffeinated beverage as prescribed. The recommended bar comes with its own added espresso assuring that you have adequate energy for your next endeavor, whether it's shopping, driving cross country or cycling 20 miles on the lunch hour.

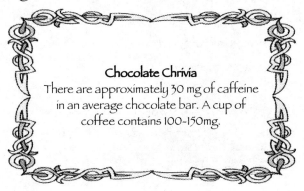

Chocolate Chrivia
There are approximately 30 mg of caffeine in an average chocolate bar. A cup of coffee contains 100-150mg.

CANCER

Prescription: 1/2 dark organic chocolate bar with or without almonds, taken daily for the rest of your life.

Recommended bar: Chocolove® dark chocolate with almonds and cherries

SUPPORTING EVIDENCE

Flavinoids are highly protective antioxidants that provide a powerful boost to the immune system. Not surprisingly flavinoids are plentiful in dark chocolate. At the University of Hawaii's Cancer Research Center, volunteers whose diets contained the highest consumption of flavinoids showed a 40-50% reduction in lung cancer. In another study in Finland, a 24-year investigation of 10,000 people confirmed that those who regularly ate the highest quantity of flavinoids showed a 20% reduction in developing all types of cancer. And at Georgetown University, a study is currently underway to test the theory that flavinoids isolated from chocolate might be used as an anti-cancer drug.

The research on antioxidants and their ability to fight cancer is abundant. Gram for gram, chocolate has a very high antioxidant content. It's an excellent choice when considering snack options to help the body fight toxins and prevent the breakdown of healthy cells. If you choose the recommended bar, you'll also gain value from the almonds. In a study done at the University of California, Davis, researchers determined that almond consumption may provide some protection against the development of colon cancer in rats. Researchers believe that colon cancer is a diet-based disease, and a diet high in fiber (present in almonds) helps reduce the possibility of developing this type of cancer.

CAVITIES

Prescription: 4 oz dark organic chocolate taken after meals and prior to brushing teeth. Chew sugar-free gum afterward to help clean teeth. Smile.

Recommended bar: Terra Nostra™ organic dark truffle

SUPPORTING EVIDENCE

Although chocolate contains sugar, it also contains phosphates and other minerals that inhibit bacteria growth formed by the sugars that promote tooth decay. The Eastman Dental Center in Rochester, New York, concluded that "...milk chocolate is one of the snack foods least likely to contribute to tooth decay."

Research also suggests that the length of time food spends in the mouth is more likely to contribute to its cavity-producing capacity and not the amount of sugar it contains. Foods like chocolate, juice and pop all exit the mouth much quicker than cookies, breads and chewier foods. The recommended bar, a truffle, is softer and will exit the mouth quicker than regular dark chocolate.

CONSTIPATION

Prescription: Microwave 1 dark organic chocolate bar on a plate for 2 minutes. Stir, then microwave for 1 additional minute or until chocolate is melted. (You may have to microwave and stir a few times to get smooth consistency.) Mix in 10 almonds, stir and allow to cool. Take 1/4 of the bar every hour with hot water or hot tea until problem is alleviated, not to exceed one bar of chocolate in a 24 hour period.

Recommended bar: Cloud Nine™ premium dark chocolate with espresso

SUPPORTING EVIDENCE

One hundred grams of chocolate contains 15g of fiber. There are also compounds in chocolate that have actually been shown to stimulate contractions of the intestinal canal. But to get the maximum benefit, I've recommended a healthy dose of almonds to compliment the chocolate prescription.

According to the California Almond Board, eating 11-15 almonds before bed will help cleanse the stomach by morning. One ounce of almonds contains 3 grams of fiber which assists the body in eliminating toxic waste. With this in mind, the prescription calls for a chocolate/almond nut bark with plenty of almonds for maximum benefits. If you choose the recommended bar, you'll also get minimal amounts of espresso. While espresso isn't normally used as a relief medication for constipation, some people report that coffee helps assist with the task at hand. However, some research advises staying away from coffee when constipated. If you find that coffee aggravates your condition, choose a bar without espresso.

COUGH

Prescription: 1 cup milk, 2 tsp dark chocolate cocoa powder, 1 tsp sugar; Mix together in a cup and microwave for 1 minute. Take as needed, with a bowl of chicken soup if preferred. Refrain from working or going to school if applicable, for at least one day.

Recommended cocoa: Rapunzel 100% organic cocoa powder

SUPPORTING EVIDENCE

Chocolate contains a stimulant called theobromine. The National Heart and Lung Institute in London recently conducted a study comparing theobromine to codeine (a popular ingredient in cough medicine) for its effectiveness in suppressing coughs. The theobromine proved to be equally as effective as the codeine. Combined with its other wonderful antioxidant and euphoric inducing components, home made chocolate milk is an excellent choice when nursing a cold.

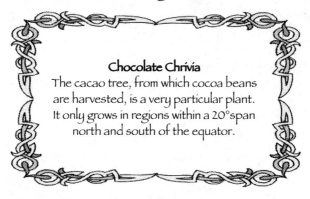

Chocolate Chrivia
The cacao tree, from which cocoa beans are harvested, is a very particular plant. It only grows in regions within a 20°span north and south of the equator.

DEPRESSION

Prescription: 4 squares dark chocolate with dried fruit, taken every hour as needed, not to exceed a maximum of 2.5 oz. in any 24 hour period. Read an uplifting novel and repeat positive affirmations between doses.

Recommended bar: Endangered Species™ dark chocolate with raspberries

SUPPORTING EVIDENCE

Chocolate has been reported to stimulate the secretion of several endorphins that are beneficial to a state of well-being. Eating chocolate may even produce the same pleasurable sensation as running several miles.

Chocolate contains both serotonin and tryptophan, neurotransmitters that act as anti-depressants in the brain. In addition, two other chemicals in chocolate, caffeine and theobromine, exhibit mood lifting effects. It's not advised to replace anti-depressant medication with chocolate, but it's acceptable to add the prescription to your program for maximum benefits.

If you select the recommended bar, you'll benefit from the dried raspberries as well. Studies comparing different populations have concluded that eating fruit may help reduce the possibility of developing a host of problems including diabetes, cataracts, heart failure, indigestion, PMS and strokes. Although none of these ailments is specifically depression, avoiding them by eating healthier foods provides considerably less reason to be depressed.

Note on prescribed positive affirmations: make sure they're positive! Affirmations should be free of negative words.

Not acceptable: I won't eat more than the prescribed chocolate for my condition.

Acceptable: I easily enjoy the right amount of chocolate for my condition.

ENERGY LOSS

Prescription: 2 squares dark organic chocolate with dried berries or other dried fruit, taken after lunch, every two hours until dinner time. After taking chocolate, take 10 deep breaths and hold for four seconds each, exhale. Maximum of 12 squares in a 24 hour period.

Recommended bar: Terra Nostra™ dark organic chocolate with raisins & pecans or Chocolove® dark organic chocolate with orange peel.

SUPPORTING EVIDENCE

The case for chocolate as an energy source lands on both sides of the fence. On one hand, chocolate contains sugar that the body quickly absorbs for energy use. But it also contains fat, which slows the absorption of these sugars into the blood. Picking up your energy level requires a quick infusion of sugar, so take into account what's been added to your chocolate when attempting to increase energy levels.

"Snickers™ really satisfies." This campaign has been so successful many people I know won't even ski or bike without a Snickers™ tucked into their jacket. But consider eating dried fruits with chocolate rather than caramel and nougat as an energy source. Approximately six pounds of fruit creates just one pound of dried fruit, and caloric and vitamin value are fully retained. The body readily absorbs the sugars in fruit, both glucose and fructose, making them an ideal choice for replenishing energy reserves. The high fiber content of fruit promotes regularity and helps keep the body free from toxic waste build up.

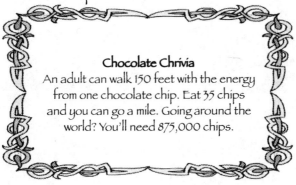

Chocolate Chrivia
An adult can walk 150 feet with the energy from one chocolate chip. Eat 35 chips and you can go a mile. Going around the world? You'll need 875,000 chips.

FLATULENCE

Prescription: 1/2 bar (1.5 oz) dark chocolate with mint. Drink one cup mint tea, take 4 mint Tic-tacs™ if needed for emergency situations.

Recommended bar: Tropical Source® mint dark chocolate

SUPPORTING EVIDENCE

While chocolate alone might not curb outbursts, the blend of chocolate with mint may be just the right combination. Mint is a stimulant that has been used for centuries as a digestive aide to counteract spasms in the digestive tract. It stimulates the flow of bile and promotes gastric secretions as well, adding to the overall digestive flow. Be sure to follow the entire prescription for an increased level of comfort, especially prior to a business meeting.

FOOD CRAVINGS

Prescription: 1 square milk chocolate, 1 square dark chocolate, one cup hot cocoa made with real cocoa powder and sugar (See Appendix C for recipe). Repeat as needed until cravings subside, up to a maximum of 2 oz. of chocolate per day.

Recommended bars: Dagoba® milk chocolate with espresso and cinnamon or Chocolove® extra dark chocolate.

SUPPORTING EVIDENCE

This is hardly a surprising statistic~more than half of all food cravings are said to involve chocolate. Another "astounding" fact~chocolate is the number one food women crave. And of those who declared chocolate to be their top craving, 75% stated that only chocolate would curb their craving. In other words, denying a craving or trying to curb it by eating something else isn't likely to work. It's better to cave into a craving and not feel guilty about it than it is to eat hundreds of additional calories trying to avoid it. Not only will it provide peace of mind, but it will keep the body healthier as well.

For example, if you eat 500 calories of sugar free cookies and low-carb chips but still want chocolate, you're over the limit by 500 calories and still left with the original craving. According to Debra Waterhouse, author of *Why Women Need Chocolate*, a chocolate craving can be satisfied by consuming just one Hershey's kiss (25 calories). Even a 10 kiss/250 calorie splurge is better than a binge on everything in sight while trying to avoid a craving.

Chocolate's perfectly balanced blend of sugar and fat uniquely affects food cravings. The body contains an amino acid peptide called galanin that stimulates the appetite. Because chocolate contains fat, it curbs the affect of galanin, reducing the need to eat. People also biologically crave fat when endorphins are low. Consumption of chocolate helps release both endorphins and serotonin into the brain. The endorphins transmit energy and feelings of euphoria, and serotonin evokes calm and mood stability.

If that's not enough to have you running to the nearest chocolate store, cocoa also contains more than 400 distinct flavor compounds. It's conceivable that by eating just one little piece of chocolate all of your extraneous cravings can be contained. In a study done on self-professed chocoholics, volunteers were given a variety of chocolates~milk, white, plain cocoa powder and a placebo. The only one that effectively satisfied the craving was milk chocolate. (They were not given dark chocolate.)

So please make a note when addressing cravings~it's best to just go right to the source of the problem. Attempting to avoid it may cause you to consume every morsel of food within a six mile radius! Follow the prescription and end the craving before monumental damage is done.

Chocolate Chrivia
A 1.5 oz milk chocolate bar contains 220 calories. A 1.75 oz bag of chips contains 230 calories. Need we even make a choice?

GOING TO THE DARK SIDE
A special section for those who need assistance converting from milk to dark chocolate.

Prescription: 2 pieces basic milk chocolate, followed directly by 2 squares high quality milk chocolate, followed directly by 2 squares high quality dark chocolate. Use guidelines in "Proper Chocolate Consumption" to insure maximum effectiveness, rinsing with a high quality merlot between chocolates. Take after the evening meal.

Recommended chocolate: 2 Hershey's kisses, Green & Black's milk chocolate with almonds, Chocolove® dark cherry almond

SUPPORTING EVIDENCE

Although it tastes delicious, milk chocolate is not the ideal choice for those who wish to obtain the significant benefits from chocolate. It contains far too many fats and sugars. Milk chocolate is like fried zucchini—the initial product in its raw form is wonderful, but by the time it gets to your mouth it's so heavily disguised it's virtually unrecognizable. If you follow this simple procedure, it won't take long to acquire a true appreciation for the darker delicacy.

The first step is to move from standard quality to high quality milk chocolate. I recommend Green & Black's as the high quality milk chocolate because it contains a higher percentage of cocoa than the average milk chocolate bar and it tastes fabulous.

For the dark chocolate, I recommend Chocolove® because their dark chocolate tastes wonderful and it's easy on the palate. This brand also offers a complete assortment of two milk and eight dark bars with the amount of cocoa they contain listed in order on the back of every bar. To simplify the entire process, use Chocolove® from start to finish to bring about the conversion. Ultimately you'll reach a point where you truly enjoy dark chocolate. Then there'll be no reason to compromise your health while enjoying your passion.

Chocolate Chrivia
Dark chocolate can be stored indefinitely in a cool, dry place (like a wine cellar). White and milk chocolate have a limited shelf life.

HEADACHE

Prescription: 1.6 oz dark organic chocolate, taken with chocolate milk made from cocoa powder and the sweetener of your choice (see recipe in Appendix C). Consume directly after a meal. Lie down for 10 minutes after consumption, elevate feet, breathe deeply.

Recommended cocoa: Ghirardelli cocoa powder for hot cocoa; Cloud Nine™ dark chocolate with raspberry chocolate bar.

SUPPORTING EVIDENCE

Consumption of dark chocolate raises the level of nitric oxide in the blood, a chemical that dilates blood vessels and allows more blood to pass through the veins. Aspirin works much the same way in the brain by expanding constricted blood vessels to reduce pain. But do you have to eat 10 chocolate bars to benefit? According to Carl Keen of the University of California nutrition department, drinking 25g of semisweet chocolate affects the blood as much as consuming an 81-miligram dose of aspirin (approximately 1/3 aspirin). Even if you don't have a headache, it's OK to play it safe and take a couple of chocolate squares after dinner just to make sure your blood is flowing.

Some studies advised against eating chocolate for those prone to headaches, especially migraines. Chocolate is rumored to act as a trigger for headaches in some cases. But it's quite possible that something else is the actual cause of the headaches in many of those studies and not the cocoa. In a double blind study at the University of Pittsburg, subjects were given chocolate and carob (a food that tastes like chocolate that doesn't contain cocoa) over a two week period. The results demonstrated little difference in chocolate and carob as migraine triggers. In fact, the researchers determined that chocolate does not appear to trigger headaches. More than one study has come to this same conclusion. Once again, when considering the research, a very dark chocolate bar is probably the best choice because it contains more nitric-oxide releasing cocoa.

HEARTBREAK

Prescription: Unlimited dark organic chocolate squares as needed. Call friends in the morning. Avoid sappy movies about lovers, sad or melancholy music, depressing books and rain.

Recommended bar: Ghirardelli sweet dark baking bar

SUPPORTING EVIDENCE

Admittedly, a prescription to eat baking chocolate is extreme. But a broken heart calls for drastic measures and the darker the better. Chocolate contains a very powerful amphetamine called phenylethylamine (PEA). PEA triggers a release of natural opiates in the brain and induces a feeling of bliss. PEA is also the same chemical the brain emits when you experience the rush of falling in love. And not surprisingly, there's even a substantial increase of PEA in the brain during orgasm.

Chocolate offers up quite a collection of positives~natural opiates, the feeling of falling in love and orgasmic bliss. Clearly it satisfies at least a few of our basic love needs without the arguments or frustration of trying to understand the opposite sex. And at a trivial few dollars or less per bar, it's a superb value when compared to $150+/hour for therapy. It's no mystery as to why it's a good idea to pamper a lovesick heart with a chocolate one.

HEART DISEASE

Prescription: 8 squares dark chocolate with almonds (or nut of your choice) for 3 days in a row after lunch, one day off, repeat as needed.

Recommended bar: Endangered Species™ dark organic chocolate with coconut and macadamia nuts or Tropical Source® toasted almond dark chocolate.

SUPPORTING EVIDENCE

Cocoa contains phytochemicals called flavinoids, a powerful type of antioxidant. Flavinoids aren't just found in chocolate~they're also found in fruits, vegetables, tea and even red wines. Recent research suggests that antioxidants help block artery damage caused by free radicals. They also block platelet aggregation in the blood, reducing the risk of heart attack and stroke. Not long ago red wine received a favorable nod as an excellent source of antioxidants. Yet a cup of hot chocolate made with two tablespoons of cocoa contains almost twice as many antioxidants as a glass of red wine.

At the University of California, researchers fed 1.6 oz. of dark chocolate per day to 22 volunteers over the course of two weeks. Half received the actual chocolate and the other half a placebo. Those who received the chocolate showed significantly more relaxation in their blood vessels than those who didn't. Better blood flow through the arteries means less clogging.

Even the Journal of American Dietetic Association reported that chocolate benefits the heart because it contains antioxidants and flavinoids. These substances help prevent cholesterol from building up in the arteries, reducing the risk of heart disease.

Adding nuts to chocolate, as prescribed, also assists the heart. Nuts are high in both monounsaturated and polyunsaturated fats~the "good" fats. Consuming nuts has actually been linked to a decrease in risk for heart attacks. A recent study at Tufts University in Boston found that the combination of a phytochemical (or anti-oxidant) found in the skin of almonds, combined with the vitamin E actually contained in almonds, protected LDL cholesterols (bad fats) from oxidation. Eating nuts has also been shown to increase HDL's or "good fats" in the bloodstream. The net result is more good fats and less bad fats.

HiGH BLOOD PRESSURE

Prescription: 4-8 squares dark organic chocolate, taken after dinner with a glass of red wine. Listen to baroque style music (60 beats per minute or slower) with both feet kicked up on the couch for a minimum of 10 minutes before proceeding with your evening plans.

Recommended bar: Dagoba® organic dark chocolate with lime & macadamia nuts

SUPPORTING EVIDENCE

Salt and high blood pressure~a cause/effect relationship that has been around for years. Yet a study done on the Kuna people, a tribe living off the coast of Panama, discovered that despite a high salt diet, their blood pressure levels were extremely low. The chocolate connection? The Kuna drink about five cups of chocolate per day. A follow up study done by Norman Hollenburg at Harvard University confirmed the possible link. Hollenburg fed volunteers both milk and dark chocolate. Those who consumed the equivalent amount of dark chocolate as the Kuna people showed a marked increase in nitric oxide in their blood. Nitric oxide relaxes and dilates blood vessels, reducing blood pressure by allowing more blood to pass through the veins.

In another interesting study, a team of Greek researchers tested artery constriction in a group of volunteers. After fasting for five hours, half of the group received 100g of chocolate (3.5 oz bar) for a snack and the other half received nothing. The researches tested both blood flow and pulse of the subjects for three hours by ultrasound. The study showed that the chocolate consumer's arteries dilated 20% more than those who had not eaten chocolate. The highest dilation occurred after three hours (the end of the test), suggesting that the benefits continued to increase even after the test was over. Once again, higher dilation of blood vessels allows more blood to pass through the veins and reduces blood pressure.

If you choose the recommended Dagoba® bar with lime and macadamia nuts, you'll benefit even more. Lime has been used for its motivating and morale boosting qualities in aromatherapy. And macadamia nuts are low in salt and high in mono-unsaturated "good fats," which helps to lower cholesterol.

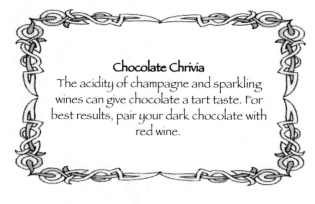

Chocolate Chrivia
The acidity of champagne and sparkling wines can give chocolate a tart taste. For best results, pair your dark chocolate with red wine.

HiGH CHOLESTEROL

Prescription: 1/2 bar high grade (60%+ cocoa) dark chocolate with nuts as part of your daily intake, taken with your afternoon latte and a whole grain bagel or crackers.

Recommended bar: Endangered Species™ dark chocolate with cranberries and almonds

SUPPORTING EVIDENCE

Eating chocolate on a regular basis may actually lower your cholesterol. While chocolate contains fat, most of it is considered healthy. Over 65% of the fats in chocolate are of the "good fat" variety. Consuming high quality chocolate has also proven to reduce the "stickiness" of platelets in the blood. This effectively lowers the level of LDL or "bad" cholesterol and allows the blood to run more efficiently through the body.

A typical dark chocolate bar contains approximately 11g of fat, more than half of it saturated. But saturated fat is actually losing ground as a "bad" fat. A study that reviewed the diets of both the Masai and Eskimo tribes showed that despite their extremely high intake of saturated fats (in meat, beef, milk and whale blubber), heart disease is virtually unknown to their cultures. The exact type of saturated fat seems to make all the difference, and chocolate primarily contains the favored fats.

A breakdown of the fat in a dark chocolate bar reveals that four grams are made up of oleic acid~the same fat found in olive oil and considered a healthy fat. Another part of the saturated fat is stearic acid, which is also converted to oleic acid by the liver. Only 25% of the fat in chocolate is palmitic acid, considered "bad fat." At the University of Pennsylvania, a study compared subjects who were given cocoa butter to another group who was given regular butter. Those who were fed cocoa butter showed no increase in cholesterol levels, while those who were given regular butter showed an increase. Despite the fact that chocolate contains a very small amount of unhealthy fat, chocolate's cholesterol friendly fats outweigh the effects of its few bad fats.

In a study conducted at Pennsylvania State University, researchers had a group of volunteers add 16g of dark chocolate and 22g of cocoa powder to their daily diet. All of the volunteers had improved cholesterol levels. Even the "bad" LDL cholesterol appeared to be more resistant to oxidation by free radicals, making it less dangerous to the heart. In a similar study, researches gave volunteers a milk chocolate bar for a snack instead of a high carbohydrate alternative (bagel, chips, etc.). The subjects' level of HDL (good fats) increased while the bad cholesterol remained unchanged, suggesting that cholesterol levels can improve by eating chocolate.

Had the researchers used high quality dark chocolate, the results would have been even more impressive.

Adding nuts to chocolate also assists the body's "good" cholesterol count. Research has confirmed that people who eat nuts on a regular basis have significantly lower levels of heart disease. Almonds and walnuts are particularly healthful. In fact, some studies have shown that eating just one ounce of almonds per day can actually lower cholesterol levels. However, even pistachios and hazelnuts have been reported to help lower cholesterol, so take your medicine!

HYPERTENSION

Prescription: 4 squares dark chocolate, taken with 4 ounces of water, not to exceed three doses of chocolate daily (more water is acceptable, of course).

Recommended bar: Endangered Species™ smooth dark chocolate

SUPPORTING EVIDENCE

Cocoa is one of the best natural sources of magnesium. Researchers have discovered a link between deficiency in this trace mineral and hypertension, heart disease and even PMS. Meeting the daily magnesium requirement has been shown to be beneficial for both the cardiovascular system and hypertension. A 3 oz bar contains 100 mg of magnesium, approximately 25% of the daily magnesium requirement. (Refer to the Vitamin Deficiency section where you'll find the complete nutrient contents of a dark chocolate bar.)

IMMUNE DEFICIENCY

Prescription: 3 squares dark organic chocolate; one cup hot cocoa made with cocoa powder and sweetener of your choice (see Appendix C), taken whenever you feel an illness coming on. Optional, 1000 mg vitamin C with dosage.

Recommendations: Endangered Species™ dark chocolate with tangerine essence. Rapunzel 100% organic baking cocoa powder.

SUPPORTING EVIDENCE

A study in Japan recently confirmed that chocolate contains phenolics. These powerful compounds have been shown to boost the immune system when tested in human blood samples. Like antioxidants, phenolics also have a proven ability to suppress body-damaging free radicals. But immune system support from chocolate doesn't end there. Dark chocolate also contains a plentiful supply of antioxidants—three times more than blueberries, a food with very high levels of antioxidants. Antioxidants assist the immune system by helping the body maintain healthy, disease-fighting cells. If you choose the recommended bar you'll also enjoy the essence of tangerine, a citrus fruit packed with vitamin C, another immune system booster.

LACK OF SEXUAL DESIRE

Prescription: One entire bar of dark organic chocolate, shared with a partner in bed while reading poetry by candle light. Optional activities when finished medicating.

Recommended bar: Chocolove® dark chocolate with almonds and cherries

SUPPORTING EVIDENCE

Not surprisingly, the research for arousing sexual desire is almost the same as that found in the *Heartbreak* category. Unfortunately, the two often go hand in hand. As previously mentioned, chocolate contains a very powerful amphetamine called phenylethylamine (PEA). PEA is the chemical emitted when people experience the rush of falling in love, and a substantial increase of PEA occurs in the brain during orgasm. Adding a little chocolate to your relationship mix is bound to produce some stimulating effects!

If you indulge in the prescribed bar you'll benefit from the almonds as well. One study maintained that eating 10-20 almonds a day invigorates sexual desire.

Chocolate Chrivia
The higher the quality of chocolate, the
louder it snaps when you break it.

LACTOSE INTOLERANCE

Prescription: 3 squares non-dairy dark chocolate taken whenever the mood strikes, up to a maximum of 9 squares per day.

Recommended bar: Tropical Source® raspberry dark chocolate, gluten and dairy free

SUPPORTING EVIDENCE

If you love milk but your body doesn't, this could be the answer for you. Researchers from the University of Rhode Island demonstrated that adding 1 ½ teaspoons of cocoa to milk reduced and sometimes even eliminated cramping and bloating in half of their lactose-intolerant subjects. Apparently chocolate stimulates the enzyme lactase which is required for lactose digestion. But the prescription still calls for dairy free chocolate to insure you don't aggravate the condition. However, if you find you've inadvertently ingested something containing lactose or milk, consider using chocolate to help ease the response. (For a complete selection of non-dairy chocolates, visit www.dolphinnatural.com.)

LiFE EXPECTANCY

Prescription: One dark organic chocolate bar of your choice daily for the rest of your life. Keep alcohol to a minimum, drive safe, relax and drink plenty of pure spring water.

Recommended bar: Green & Black's Maya Gold dark organic chocolate with spices

SUPPORTING EVIDENCE

Thanks to Harvard for supplying the chocolate lovers of the world with this invaluable information. After studying 7,841 male graduates, the Harvard School of Public Health reported that those who eat chocolate live nearly a year longer than those who attempt to go through life without the luxury. Although they didn't outright report it, I suspect that the real reason chocolate lovers live an extra year is so they can enjoy chocolate for another 365 days. This could quite possibly be the single most important reason to make sure there's adequate chocolate in your diet. You'll average an extra year to enjoy the fruits of the cocoa bean in its many varied splendors, as well as anything else you like to do.

Chocolate Chrivia
Napoleon reportedly carried chocolate
with him on a regular basis, eating it
whenever he needed quick energy.

MEMORY LOSS

Prescription: 4 squares dark organic chocolate, taken after lunch and again right before bed. May take with tea, water or hot chocolate (made from cocoa powder, see Appendix C).

Recommended bar: Rapunzel's Bittersweet Chocolate

SUPPORTING EVIDENCE

Memory experts have shown that eating a little of the right kind of chocolate each day can actually help improve your memory. Dark chocolate contains a compound called procyanidin that helps block the effect of two aging factors in the brain: oxidation and inflammation. These same procyanidins may also help the memory by stimulating circulation in the brain. The increased blood flow delivers more oxygen and nutrients to the brain, which helps maintain optimal function. Once again, choose the correct type of chocolate: dark chocolate containing 50% cocoa or more.

MOOD SWINGS

Prescription: 6 squares dark organic chocolate taken with or without nuts twice daily at the onset of any bad mood. It's acceptable to count picking up kids' clothes and an overstuffed garage as possible attitude triggers.

Recommended bar: Green & Black's dark organic chocolate with orange and spices

SUPPORTING EVIDENCE

There's a bounty of scientific evidence supporting the fact that the body releases endorphins (natural feel-good chemicals) when we eat chocolate. But many of the sensations we experience are difficult to document.

The mood-lifting benefits can probably best be described as a combination of events. Many people associate chocolate with love because it is generally given on Valentine's Day. You've probably received chocolate from someone who loves you even when it wasn't a special holiday. People associate good feelings with chocolate when it's consumed, and sometimes even by the mere sight of it. Chocolate also melts perfectly at body temperature. Once it's in the mouth, the smooth, creamy texture feels soft, warm and delicious, obviously initiating more feel-good sensations. The fat content in chocolate provides satiation for the appetite, and its flavor compounds satisfy a diverse assortment of cravings. When attempting to manage moods, this delightful mélange provides an abundance of support!

Chocolate Chrivia
European researchers discovered that you're more likely to catch a mouse with chocolate than with cheese.

NAUSEA / SPEAKING IN PUBLIC

Prescription: 1.6 oz (1/2 bar) dark organic chocolate, taken with 1 cup mint tea. Take peppermint mints shortly before speaking engagements. Look in the mirror prior to stepping on the podium to insure a chocolate-free face and reduce the possibility of embarrassment.

Recommended bar: Tropical Source® mint crunch dark chocolate

SUPPORTING EVIDENCE

Chocolate releases both serotonin and tryptophan into the brain, two neurotransmitters that promote relaxation. Since a relaxed state of mind is ideal for public speaking, a good quality dark chocolate bar can be very helpful. Adding mint offers additional relief as it has been used for centuries as a digestive aide. It's been used to reduce morning sickness, menstrual cramps and nausea, including the type induced by public speaking engagements. Even after a night of heavy drinking, try this prescription for measurable relief.

OSTEOPOROSIS

Prescription: 4 squares organic milk chocolate (with or without almonds) and one cup hot cocoa (see Appendix C), taken mid-morning 4-5 days per week.

Recommended bar: Dagoba® milk chocolate with ginger and chai or Organic Swiss dark chocolate with almonds.

SUPPORTING EVIDENCE

Chocolate contains both calcium and magnesium~two minerals that are deficient in many people's diets. You can't prevent osteoporosis by consuming immense quantities of chocolate. However, by following the prescription exactly, the odds of becoming calcium deficient can be moved in your favor. The cup of milk provides 30% of your daily calcium requirement, and chocolate contains minerals that assist the body with calcium absorption.

There are two chocolate bar options in the prescription~one with and one without almonds. Almonds provide an excellent collection of minerals associated with building bone density~calcium, magnesium, manganese and phosphorous. Regardless of which bar you choose, drink it with the prescribed chocolate milk for maximum benefits.

Chocolate Chrivia
Consumers spend more than $7 billion per year on chocolate.

PMS

Prescription: on days 14-25 of your cycle, take 1/4 of a 3.5 oz high quality dark chocolate bar daily after lunch, or whenever food cravings hit, limiting intake to one half bar per day. On days 25-28, consume up to an entire bar per day, as needed, to curb cravings, crabbiness and lethargy.

Recommended bar: Green & Black's dark organic chocolate

SUPPORTING EVIDENCE

Studies have shown that many women use chocolate to self-medicate during this often stressful time of the month. This is hardly breaking news. I don't know of a woman who *doesn't* use chocolate during this time of the month! There's no need to examine the reasons we use it. A simple review of many of the other ailments in this book will address the issue. After all, it appears that PMS is a collective compilation of symptoms packed into 3-5 days.

One of the actual causes of PMS is a drop in the hormone progesterone. The change can cause nasty mood swings, hot flashes, and a host of other miserable symptoms. Adding the trace mineral magnesium to the diet of those affected with chronic PMS symptoms has shown to help alleviate the problem by increasing the pre-menstrual progesterone levels. Chocolate has one of the highest concentrations of natural magnesium. Perhaps this is the real reason why many women report that they crave chocolate for days before the monthly event.

Serotonin also drops during the course of the month. It maintains a fairly normal level until approximately day 14, when it begins a steady downward path. By the last few days of the cycle, serotonin levels are at their lowest. This creates a more pronounced desire for something that will lift your mood like chocolate, which helps release serotonin into your system.

Endorphins also fly up and down the chart during the month. They actually spike within 48 hours of ovulation, toppling back down to a normal level toward the end of the cycle. The disheartening synopsis: Not only does the body experience a drop in progesterone and serotonin by month's end, but it also suffers the withdrawals of endorphin euphoria. Fortunately chocolate contains natural endorphins that can help ease this drop.

Since chocolate helps curb both the mental and physiological symptoms of PMS, be prepared! Have plenty of high quality, dark organic chocolate on hand at all times. Better to snap off the corner of a chocolate bar than your significant other's head. Do the right thing!

SASSY KIDS

Prescription: 1/2 bar of high quality dark or milk chocolate, with or without nuts, given as needed, preferably after meals or as an award for improved behavior.

Recommended bar: Dagoba® milk chocolate or Dagoba® milk chocolate with hazelnuts.

SUPPORTING EVIDENCE

Controlling children through manipulation with chocolate rewards may not seem like the best idea at first glance. But many people already use food-based rewards to encourage good behavior. The issue is more about the type of food given, not whether to give chocolate.

Kids usually act out when they're tired, hungry or in a bad mood. Chocolate offers an excellent one-two remedy with its perfect blend of sugar and fat. Sugar encourages the release of serotonin, a chemical that creates calmness and mood stability. Fat helps release endorphins, natural brain chemicals that promote energy and euphoria. Add that to all the other benefits they'll get from chocolate~vitamins, minerals, antioxidants and a host of flavor compounds and you've just solved a problem with a healthy treat. Of course kids may get the picture and act out more often in an attempt to get more chocolate. To overcome this possible hazard, just give them a few squares every day to regulate mood swings and promote euphoria (for the kids as well as the parents).

Note: I've recommended milk chocolate for kids because it's so much milder than dark chocolate. However, don't hesitate to give the little darlings dark chocolate if they like it.

Chocolate Chrivia
Chocolate was consumed exclusively as a drink for many centuries. Brittish chocolate maker J.S. Fry and Sons is credited with creating the first solid chocolate in 1830.

SNIFFLES

Prescription: 3-6 squares dark organic chocolate with mint, taken daily just after a chicken soup lunch, until symptoms subside. Maximum of 12 squares in a 24 hour period.

Recommended bar: Tropical Source® mint crunch dark chocolate

SUPPORTING EVIDENCE

Colds need plenty of pampering and chocolate with mint is just the "mother" you need. The antioxidants in chocolate help your immune system combat colds. The sugar/fat combination, assortment of flavors and endorphins will certainly make you feel better. Adding mint to your chocolate helps because peppermint relaxes breathing passages. Peppermint is used in many teas to combat nasal congestion, stuffiness, hay fever, sinusitis and allergies by helping to restore breathing.

If you're still not convinced that eating chocolate will help, consider this: More than one study has proven that placebos (usually sugar pills) are very often as effective as real medication in many areas including migraines, cancer, and even surgery. The simple idea that you "think" chocolate is helping in fact makes it so. So even if you're skeptical, take a chance and make your placebo as tasty as possible.

SPOUSAL DISCORD

Prescription: Enjoy Chocolate Kahlua® Truffles (recipe in Appendix C) and ice cream together with candles, soft music and a glass of red wine each. Children in the area will most likely counteract the effects of the prescription, so it's best to follow it in a lowly lit, private location.

SUPPORTING EVIDENCE

Chocolate, love, passion and romance. Are they rightfully bundled in the same package? It's a little difficult to prove scientifically, but the facts seem to point in that direction. Chocolate helps release feel-good chemicals in the brain, and it even contains the same chemical (PEA) that the brain emits when falling in love. It contains tryptophan and serotonin, two neurotransmitters that help the body relax and promote euphoria. And finally, with its unique sugar/fat combination, sensual melt at body temperature and the vast array of rich, complex, velvety flavors, chocolate *is* passion. Here are a few recommendations to help you reconnect with your loved one:

If you need to say:

"I Love You" A bar of high grade dark organic chocolate and a red rose across the top.

"I'm Sorry" A larger bar of high quality dark organic chocolate and a thoughtful apology on a handmade card.

"Let's Have Fun" An exotically flavored large dark chocolate bar that can be broken into individual squares and fed to your partner, as needed, while playing games of intimacy.

"You are the best person in the world!" Decorate your significant other's office (or favorite room) with various types of chocolate wrapped in colorful paper. Place a copy of "The Chocolate Therapist," tied with a tastefully selected ribbon, on the center of their desk. Follow your intuition.

STRESS

Prescription: 1/2 bar (1.0 oz) dark organic chocolate bar consumed directly after lunch every Monday when stress is likely to be at a high point. Repeat as needed through the week, but always on Monday.

Recommended bar: Dagoba® organic dark chocolate with dried berries and vanilla

SUPPORTING EVIDENCE

Chocolate contains potassium and magnesium as well as several vitamins~B1, B2, D and E. The B-vitamins become depleted in the body under stressful situations. Eating a good quality chocolate bar can help replenish the nutrients lost during stress.

Chocolate promotes the release of endorphins and serotonin, natural chemicals in the brain that promote calm and euphoric feelings. There's also a substance in chocolate called anandamide which stimulates the same areas of the brain that marijuana does. Anandamide actually stays in the brain longer, prolonging the relaxed sensation in a completely safe and natural way. But no need for concern~a person would have to consume 25 pounds of chocolate to receive the same "high" as smoking one joint. Fortunately it looks as though chocolate will remain a legal substance for many years to come.

When you select the recommended bar, you'll also add the benefits of vanilla essence. This scent is used in aromatherapy to calm and relax the body.

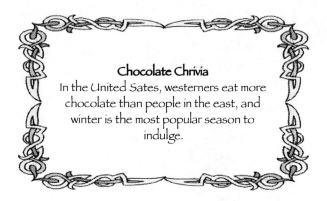

Chocolate Chrivia
In the United Sates, westerners eat more chocolate than people in the east, and winter is the most popular season to indulge.

SUGAR OVERLOAD

Prescription: 1/2 bar of the strongest dark chocolate you can tolerate, preferably 70% organic cocoa or higher. Take one dose daily to curb sugar cravings. Strictly avoid candies with dyes, as they're almost always pure sugar.

Recommended bar: Chocolove® extra dark chocolate

SUPPORTING EVIDENCE

Without sugar most people can't tolerate the bitterness of chocolate, so the two are regularly found together. But if you're trying to avoid or reduce sugar, it stands to reason that a new plan of *more* chocolate will never work. However, a good quality dark chocolate bar doesn't contain nearly as much sugar as some of the other, more "acceptable" snacks. After comparing the grams of sugar in the listed foods, you may want to reconsider allowing chocolate back into the snack cupboard.

Grams of Sugar per Serving

Chocolove Extra Dark Chocolate bar	9 g
1/3 cup Craisins	26 g
1 Cup Life Cereal / Dry	12 g
16 oz Gatorade	26 g
Nature Valley Chewy Granola Bar	13 g
Coca Cola / 1 can	27 g
1 Small Hershey's Brownie	17 g
Yoplait Fat Free Yogurt	15 g

Many people I interviewed agreed that it's difficult to completely eliminate sugar from the diet, especially when beginning a new diet and attempting to go cold turkey. Sugar appears to have addictive qualities, probably more psychological than physical. When you're starting a new diet, try using very dark chocolate to avert cravings or binges triggered by sugar withdrawal (see Food Cravings for additional information). Even if you're not starting a diet, adding a little dark chocolate to your day is bound to offer some pleasurable assistance.

WEIGHT GAIN

Prescription: Use high quality dark chocolate with nuts, as needed to curb food cravings and hunger. Eat 2-3 squares at a time, not to exceed a maximum of one 2 oz bar per day. Take a 20-30 minute walk 4 evenings per week.

Recommended bar: Organic Swiss dark chocolate with almonds

SUPPORTING EVIDENCE

Because it's rumored to contain fat, chocolate may be the most feared weapon in the diet universe. But chocolate is responsible for less than 2% of the fat in the American diet. The majority of our dietary fat actually comes from meat, dairy products and fried foods. Recent research has uncovered a surprising collection of facts that debunk many of the myths about chocolate, fats and getting fat.

As mentioned in the Food Craving section, the body contains an appetite stimulant called galanin. The fat in chocolate curbs the effects of galanin, reducing the need to eat. Most of the fat in chocolate is considered "healthy fat" which helps raise good HDL cholesterol and lower bad LDL cholesterol. If you're counting calories or fat grams, compare the calories in one bar of chocolate to other snack prospects.

Food	Cal	Fat Content	Carbs
Dagoba dark w/Lime And Macadamia nuts	156	6g	15g
1/2 c. ice-cream Ben & Jerry's Chubby Hubby	350	21g	33g
2 Granola Bars Nature's Valley	180	6g	29g

McD's Crispy Chicken Sandwich	500	26g	46g
Krispy Kreme glazed donut	210	12g	22g
11 Hershey's Kisses	275	4.5g	9g
2 dark Lindt truffles	140	12g	10g

Chocolate also comes in very low on the glycemic index (GI) chart. Low GI foods are optimal for weight loss because they don't raise blood sugar very much (see appendix D for more info on the glycemic index). Lower blood sugar means lower levels of insulin in the blood, and when insulin stays out the fat stays off. To maintain the lowest levels of insulin, consume chocolate after meals rather than as a snack between meals.

Worried about the nut calories in the prescribed bar? More than one study has concluded that adding hundreds of nut calories to the diet over a six-month period does not add weight. Even when you eat enough nuts to finally induce weight gain, the actual gain does not correspond to the expected outcome for the increased caloric intake. Since nuts contain so much fiber, it's quite possible that they aren't completely digested. Fiber also helps the body rid itself excess pounds by encouraging the release of excrement.

Eating chocolate will not cause excessive weight gain. But eating too many calories and not getting enough exercise will definitely pack on the pounds. Almost anything eaten in excess will cause weight gain whether it's fat free ice cream, whole grain pasta or low-carb crackers with cheese. The key is moderation. Chocolate can assist this goal by suppressing the appetite, containing food cravings and offering plenty of vitamins, minerals and mood-stabilizing endorphins to the body.

Chocolate Chrivia
Fifty-two percent of Americans claim chocolate as their favorite flavor. Vanilla and berry flavors tie for second.

VITAMIN DEFICIENCY

Prescription: 3 squares dark organic chocolate with breakfast three days per week, along with your daily vitamins.

Recommended bar: Dagoba® dark chocolate with dried berries and vanilla

SUPPORTING EVIDENCE

The following chart shows the nutrient contents of a dark chocolate bar. I compared the fat and calorie values for the listed bar to the chocolate bars recommended throughout the book, and it's clear that the bar used for this information is inferior to the bars in the book. Researchers didn't specify the exact type of chocolate used, but had they used a higher quality dark chocolate bar, the results of this chart would be even more encouraging. None-the-less, it's interesting to note the extensive inventory of nutrients in a single bar.

Nutrients in dark chocolate

Nutrient	Units	Value/100g	1 bar/44g
Energy	Kcal	479	210.76
Protein	G	4.20	1.85
Total lipid (fat)	G	30	13.20
Carbohydrate	G	63.10	27.76
Fiber, dietary	G	5.9	2.60
Sugars, total	G	54.50	23.98
Calcium	Mg	32.00	14.08
Iron, Fe	Mg	3.13	1.38
Magnesium, Mg	Mg	115.00	50.60
Phosphorus, P	Mg	132.00	58.08
Potassium, K	Mg	365.00	160.60
Sodium, Na	Mg	11.00	4.84
Zinc, Zn	Mg	1.62	0.71
Copper, Cu	Mg	0.70	0.31
Manganese, Mn	Mg	.80	0.35
Selenium, Se	Mcg	3.10	1.36
Vitamin C	Mg	0.00	0.00
Thiamin	Mg	0.06	0.02
Riboflavin	Mg	0.09	0.04
Niacin	Mg	0.43	0.19
Pantothentic Acid	Mg	0.11	0.05
Vitamin B-6	Mg	0.034	0.02
Vitamin A, IU	IU	21.00	9.24
Vitamin A, RE	Mcg_RE	2.00	0.88
Vitamin E	Mg_ATE	1.19	0.52
Fatty acids, sat	G	17.75	7.81
Fatty acids, unsat	G	0.97	0.43
Cholesterol	Mg	0	0
Caffeine	Mg	62.00	22.28
Theobromine	Mg	486.00	213.84

USDA Nutrient Database for Standard Reference, Release 13
(November 1999)

If you select the recommended bar, you'll also benefit from the vitamin C contained in dried cherries, as well as the pleasing and relaxing aroma of the vanilla beans.

WRAPPING IT UP

The story of chocolate is a mirror of itself—rich, complex, mysterious and enjoyable. It was a "food of the Gods" for the Aztecs, an aphrodisiac for Montezuma and a highly guarded secret of Spanish aristocracy. Today, this once guilty pleasure has turned in to the latest necessity for health.

Research continues to unveil the hidden benefits of chocolate every day. New companies offering unique and quality chocolate are racing to the scene to capitalize on the action. Discriminating consumers are driving the ascent of quality chocolate world-wide.

The world is ready for the next chocolate revolution: Top quality chocolate available everywhere at affordable prices! It's time for vitamin enhanced chocolate teas, lattes, beer, wine and sodas! Dark chocolate covered fruits and vegetables at convenience store counters!

Dark chocolate yogurt, vitamin enhanced chocolate bars and organic chocolate protein smoothies! If dark chocolate isn't on your menu, it's time to renovate your plan. Out with the chips and in with chocolate. Snacking has never been healthier!

A simple chocolate bar may have satisfied the cravings of a sheltered youth, but things are different now. The twenty-first century chocolate connoisseur demands tasteful perfection. Why stop now? Educate yourself, demand excellence, eat chocolate and stay happy.

APPENDIX A / CHOCOLATE WEBSITES

www.chocolatebar.com
www.chocolateinfo.com
www.chocolove.com
www.chocolatetradingcompany.com
www.chocosphere.com
www.cloudnineconfections.com
www.dagobachocolate.com
www.diamondorganic.com/chocolate
www.eccobella.com
www.exploratorium.edu
www.ghirardelli.com
www.godiva.com
www.greenandblacks.com
www.newmansownorganics.com
www.nspiredfoods.com
www.organic-chocolates.com
www.rapunzel.com
www.romolochocolates.com
www.terranostra.us
www.valrhona.com
www.venussweets.com
www.worldwidechocolate.com

APPENDIX B / RECOMMENDED CHOCOLATE BARS

Brand	Description	Size
Chocolove	Dark Choc w/Almonds & Cherry	3.2 oz
Chocolove	Extra Dark Chocolate	3.2 oz
Chocolove	Orange Peel w/Dark Chocolate	3.2 oz
Cloud Nine	Premium Dark Choc w/Espresso	2.0 oz
Cloud Nine	Dark Chocolate w/Raspberry	2.0 oz
Dagoba Dark	Chocolate w/Lime & Macadamia	2.0 oz
Dagoba Dark	Chocolate w/dried berry & vanilla	2.0 oz
Dagoba Milk	Chocolate with hazelnuts	2.0 oz
Dagoba Dark	Chocolate w/lavender & blueberry	2.0 oz
Dagoba Milk	Chocolate w/ginger and chai	2.0 oz
Dagoba Milk	Chocolate w/espresso & cinnamon	2.0 oz
Endangered Species	Smooth Dark Chocolate	3.0 oz
Endangered Species	Dark Chocolate w/Espresso	3.0 oz
Endangered Species	Dark Chocolate w/Raspberries	3.0 oz
Endangered Species	Organic Dark w/Tangerine Ess	1.4 oz
Endangered Species	Organic Dark w/Cherry Ess	1.4 oz
Endangered Species	Dark Chocolate w/Blueberries	3.0 oz
Endangered Species	Dark Chocolate w/Cran & Almo	3.0 oz
Endangered Species	Dark Organic w/Coconut & Mac	3.0 oz
Ghirardelli	Sweet Dark Baking Bar	4.0 oz
Ghirardelli	Semi-Sweet Baking Bar	4.0 oz
Green & Black	Organic Dark Chocolate	3.5 oz
Green & Black	Maya Gold-Org Dark w/Spices	3.5 oz
Green & Black	Organic Dark w/Orange and Spices	3.5 oz
Godiva	Dark Chocolate w/Raspberry	1.5 oz

Newman's Own	Organic Sweet Dark w/Espresso	1.2 oz
Newman's Own	Organic Sweet Dark w/Espresso	2.8 oz
Organic Swiss	Dark Chocolate	3.0 oz
Organic Swiss	Dark Chocolate with Almonds	3.0 oz
Rapunzel	Bittersweet Chocolate	3.0 oz
Rapunzel	Semisweet Chocolate	3.0 oz
Rapunzel	Semisweet w/Hazelnuts	3.0 oz
Terra Nostra	Organic Intense Dark Chocolate	3.5 oz
Terra Nostra	Organic Dark w/Raisins	3.5 oz
Terra Nostra	Organic Dark Truffle	3.5 oz
Tropical Source	Mint Crunch Dark Chocolate	3.0 oz
Tropical Source	Toasted Almond Dark Chocolate	3.0 oz
Tropical Source	Raspberry Dark Chocolate	3.0 oz

Most brands are carried at natural food stores like Whole Foods and Wild Oats. Some of the more popular brands like Newman's Own® and Green & Black's are also carried at regular grocery stores. Any brand of organic dark chocolate will work for the prescriptions. Don't hold back if you can't find the exact bar that's prescribed~just go with your favorite or the brand that's available.

APPENDIX C / RECIPES

If you have an original chocolate recipe that you'd like featured in my next book, please e-mail it to:

recipes@thechocolatetherapist.com

Include your full name and a note with your permission to reprint the recipe.

HOT CHOCOLATE (RAPUNZEL COCOA POWDER BOX)

1 cup milk
1-1/2 tsp sugar or sugar substitute if preferred
2 tsp Rapunzel 100% organic cocoa powder (or brand of your choice)
1 drop vanilla, sprinkle of cinnamon optional

Mix together in a cup and microwave for 1 minute, 40 seconds. Or mix together in a pan and heat slowly over the stove, stirring constantly, until desired heat is reached.

CHOCOLATE KAHLUA® TRUFFLES (KRISTIN RENZEMA)

12 oz semi-sweet dark organic chocolate chips
1/2 cup heavy cream (NOT half and half)
1/2 stick butter (do not use margarine)
1 Tablespoon instant coffee granules
2 Tablespoons Kahlua®
1/2 tsp of salt
cocoa powder for dusting

Combine all ingredients (except cocoa powder) in small saucepan. Heat over low heat, stirring occasionally until very smooth. Chill until firm. Roll into 1" balls, and roll in cocoa powder. Store in refrigerator or freezer for up to 1 month.

RASPBERRY TRUFFLE BROWNIES (KRISTIN RENZEMA)

3/4 cup butter
4 ounces dark organic unsweetened chocolate, chopped
3 large eggs
2 cups sugar
1/3 cup raspberry jam
3 Tablespoons black raspberry liqueur (such as Chateau Monet Framboise)
1 cup all purpose flour
1/4 teaspoon salt
1 cup Ghirardelli™ double chocolate chips

Preheat oven to 350°. Spray 9 inch diameter spring form pan with nonstick spray. Melt butter and chocolate in large saucepan over low heat, stirring until smooth. Remove from heat. Whisk in eggs, sugar, jam and liqueur. Stir in flour and salt, then chocolate chips. Transfer batter to prepared pan.

Bake brownie until tester (toothpick) inserted comes out with moist crumbs attached, about 45 minutes. Cool in pan on rack. Run small knife around edges of pan. Remove pan sides. Dust with powdered sugar. Cut into 12 wedges.

CHOCOLATE MOUSSE (DEETTE KOZLOW)

6 oz. Green & Black's extra dark organic chocolate
3 Tbs Grand Marnier®
1-1/4 cup milk
5 large eggs, separated
2 Tbs sugar

Chop chocolate into small pieces and combine with Grand Marnier® in a small sauce pan. Heat slowly over hot water until melted. In another sauce pan, heat milk until not quite boiling. In a bowl, wisk egg yolks and 2 Tbs sugar until light, slowly add hot milk. Return to sauce pan and place over simmering water. Stir until it thickens and coats spoon. Take from heat, gradually stir in melted chocolate. In a bowl, beat egg whites until foamy. Add 1 Tbs sugar and continue beating until stiff. Carefully fold into chocolate mixture. Pour into dessert cups, chill several hours. Serves 6-8.

CHOCOLATE DROP COOKIES (LIANNE MCCRIRICK)

2 eggs, beaten
1 cup butter
1 cup milk
2 cups brown sugar
4 cups flour (sift together w/soda)
1 tsp baking soda
4 squares dark organic baking chocolate, melted
1/2 c. chopped walnuts

Cream sugar and butter, add eggs and chocolate, then add milk. Blend together well. Add flour and soda mixture and stir. Drop from spoon onto baking sheet and bake approx 10 minutes at 350°. Optional: Dust lightly with dark cocoa powder and powdered sugar mix after baking.

CHOCOLATE / CHOCOLATE-CHIP OATMEAL COOKIES (JULIE PECH)

1/2 c. shortening
1/4 c. butter
1 c brown sugar
1/2 c white sugar
2 tsp vanilla
2 eggs
1-1/4 cup flour
1/4 cup dark organic cocoa powder
1 tsp baking soda
1-1/2 tsp salt

3 c. regular oats (not quick-cooking)
2 3.5 oz Green & Black's Dark organic bars, chopped
3/4 c. pecans, chopped

Combine first 5 ingredients (shortening through vanilla) and
mix until blended. Add eggs and blend well. Add flour, salt
and soda, blend well. Add oats and blend. Add nuts and
chocolate chips. Drop onto lightly greased cookie sheet and
bake at 335° for 8-9 minutes.

APPENDIX D / THE GLYCEMIC INDEX, QUICKLY

The glycemic index is a measure of the rate at which foods affect blood sugar levels. It's been around for quite a long time, but gained popularity after the release of a book called *The Glucose Revolution: Life Plan*, and more recently *The South Beach Diet*. Carbohydrates that break down quickly have a higher glycemic index (GI) rating because they raise blood sugar levels quickly. Foods that take longer to break down have lower GI values because they raise blood sugar levels more slowly. When your blood sugar goes up, insulin is released into the bloodstream to bring sugar levels back down to a normal level. However, insulin works double duty as it's also the hormone that helps deposit fat onto our bodies. Eating a diet filled with low GI foods keeps the insulin out of the bloodstream, and this helps keep the fat off. Fortunately chocolate, especially when combined with nuts, comes in at a very low 33 on the glycemic index.

Glycemic index ratings range from 1 to 100. To keep blood sugar (and therefore insulin levels) at an ideal level, a person should try to eat foods that range between 0-60. However, if you eat a high and a low food together, the two will balance each other and the net affect is a rating somewhere in between the two. I've listed a few popular snack choices below, but for a full glycemic index chart and a complete description of how you can use the index to help control weight, please refer to *The Glucose Revolution: Life Plan*.

Snack option	Glyemic Index Rating
Bagel, 1 small plain, 2 oz	48
Grapes, 1 cup	46
Banana, 1 medium, 5 oz	55
Orange, 1 medium	44
Blueberry Muffin, 2 oz	59
Watermelon, 1 cup	72
White bread, 1 slice	70
Jelly Beans, 10 large	80
Cheerios, 1 cup, 1 oz	74
Life Cereal, 1 cup	66
Oatmeal, Old Fashioned, 1/2 c.	49
Mars Bar	65
Cantaloupe, 1/4 small	65
Oat Bran Muffin	60

Coca Cola, 1 can	63
Fettuccine, 1 cup	32
Cocoa Crispies, 1 cup	77
Vermicelli, 1 cup	35
Shortbread cookies, 4 pieces	64
Popcorn, 1.75 oz	55
Cranberry Juice, 8 oz.	52
Pretzels, 1 oz.	83
Chocolate Milk, 8 oz	34
Snickers Bar	41
French Fries, large, 4.3 oz	75
Skittles	70
Twix Chocolate Bar	44
Yogurt, with sugar 8 oz	33
Chocolate Bar, 1.5 oz.	49*
Peanut M & M's, 1.7 oz	33

*The chocolate bar listed is NOT made from dark organic chocolate. I contacted the authors of The Glucose Revolution for information on dark chocolate, but it wasn't readily available. However, they did note that all chocolate comes in quite low on the index because it contains fat, which slows its absorption into the bloodstream. A dark chocolate bar with nuts comes in even lower.

REFERENCES

"About Dried Fruit: Nutritional Information." Dried Fruit Information Services. May 16, 2004. www.driedfruit-info.com. Path: About Dried Fruit; Nutritional Information.

"Almond." Body Mind Revival. May 16, 2004. www.bodymindrevival.com. Path: Remedies with Whole Foods; Almond.

"Almonds~At the Heart of a Healthful Diet." The Almond Board of California. May 16, 2004. www.almondsarein.com. Path: Coronary Heart Disease.

"Benefits of Chocolate." Le Vie en Chocolat. May 16, 2004. www.levien-chocolat.com Path: Chocolate Benefits.

"The Beneficial, Balanced Scent of Lavender." Tomi Gion. August 31, 2004. www.tomigion.com. Path: www.tomigion.com/phpshop/sun_tip12.html.

Brand-Miller, Jennie; Burani, Johanna; Foster-Powerll, Kaye. The Glucose Revolution Life Plan. New York, Marlowe and Company, 2000

"Chocolate!" National Confection Association. March 15, 2005. www.cany-usa.org. Path: Chocolate Trivia.

"Chocolate: Facts and Fiction." The American Dietetic Association Center for Nutrition and Dietetics. Sept. 21, 2004. www.eatright.org. Path: Food and Nutrition Information; Nutrition Fact Sheets; Chocolate.

"Chocolate: The Latest Health Food." Your Pure Life. May 1, 2005. www.yourpurelife.com. Path: Articles; Healthy Living; Chocolate.

"Chocolate: Rich in History." Chocolate Source. May 20, 2005. www.chocolatesource.com. Path: About Chocolate; History.

"Chocolate Facts." Chocolate Information Center. Mars, Inc. Sept 21, 2004. www.chocolateinfo.com. Path: Chocolate Facts; Chocolate and Flavinoids.

"Chocolate's Benefits." Chef Norm's Recipe Collection. May 14, 2004. www.chefnorm.com Path: Chocolate's Benefits.

"Chocolate Benefits." WTAJ TV, Health Facts. May 16, 2004. www.wtajtx.com Path: www.wtajtx.com/health/chocbene.html.

"Chocolate Project Page." Academic Research for Computer and Higher Education Services. May 16, 2004.www.arches.uga.edu Path: www.arches.uga.edu/~cmhup/project.html.

"Chocolate Trivia." Godiva Chocolatier. May 20, 2005. www.godiva.com. Path: Recipes; Chocolate Trivia and Glossary.

Coe, Sophie D and Michael D. The True History of Chocolate. New York: Thames and Hudson, Inc. 1996.

DolphinNaturals.com. Dolphin Natural Chocolates. Oct. 14, 2004. www.dolphinnatural.com. Path: About Chocolate.

"Economics of Cocoa." ZChocolat. May 15, 2005. www.zchocolate.com.

Foreman, Judy. "Cinnamon Joins Cholesterol Battle." The Boston Globe. Aug. 24, 2004.

"Fun Facts about Chocolate." Chocolate Manufacturers Association. May 3, 2005. www.chcolateusa.org. Path: About Chocolate; Facts, Trivia.

"Ginger." Whole Health Md. August 31, 2004. www.wholehealthmd.com. Path: Reference Library; Foods; Ginger.

"Health Benefits." In tem pe ran tia May 16, 2004. www.intemperantia.com. Path: Health Benefits.

"Health Benefits (of Blueberries)." Blueberry Hills Farms. August 31, 2003. www.wildaboutberries.com. Path: Health Benefits.

"Health Benefits of Macadamia Nuts." Maloha Macadamia Nut Company. Sept 7, 2004. www.maloha.com. Path: Health Benefits.

"The Health Benefits of Chocolate." Aphrodite Handmade English Luxury Chocolates. May 16, 2004. www.aphrodite-chocolates.co.uk. Path: Chocolate Health Benefits.

"Healthy Chocolate 'Imminent'"; Los Angeles Times. February, 2004.

Health Security; IMPAKT Health, Botanical Profile: Peppermint, August 2004.

"Here's to Your Health and Happiness: Toasting the Benefits and Pleasures of Chocolate." Romolo Chocolates. May 16, 2004. www.romolochocolates.com Path: The Candy Dish; Here's to Your Health and Happiness.

"Hot Cocoa Tops Red Wine and Tea in Antioxidants: May be a Healthier Choice." Science Daily. May 25, 2005. www.sciencedaily.com. Path: www.sciencedaily.com/releases/2003/11/03/031106051159.htm.

Jacobsen, Rowan. Chocolate Unwrapped. Vermont: Invisible Cities Press, 2003

"List of High Fiber Foods." Max Labs. May 16, 2004. www.highfiberfoods.net.

"Market Trends: U.S. Gourmet Chocolate Market." Market Research. June 3, 2004. www.marketresearch.com (April 2004). Path: Food:Confectionary; market Trends: U.S. Gourmet Chocolate Market.

"Mint Comments and Uses." Tao Herb Farm. May 16, 2004. www.taoherbfarm.com. Path: Herbs; Mint.

"Nuts—The Surprising Health Benefits." Porphyry's People. Sept. 7, 2004. www.vegan.org.nz. Path: Nuts

"Pantry, The: Chocolate and Cocoa." Baking911. April 29, 2005. www.baking911.com. Path: Pantry; Chocolate; Introduction.

Seligson, FH, Krummel, DA, and Apgar, JL. "Patterns of Chocolate Consumption." The American Journal of Clinical Nutrition. May 20, 2005. www.acjn.orn.

Somer, Elizabeth. "Crazy for Chocolate." Elizabeth Somer.com. Aug. 13, 2004. www.elizabethsomer.com/eindex.php.

Talan, Jamie. "Dark Chocolate May Protect Your Heart." Atlanta Journal Constitution. June 2, 2004.

Tealand.com. May 16, 2004. www.tealand.com. Path: Seasonal Conditions; Herbal Nasal Decongestant.

Vitacost.com. May 16, 2004. www.vitacost.com. Path: Categories; Tea and Coffee; Alvita Peppermint Tea.

Waterhouse, Debra. Why Women Need Chocolate. New York, Debra Waterhouse, 1995.

ISBN 1-41204742-0